Science Discoveries

GALILEO

and the Universe

Steve Parker

Belitha Press

First published in Great Britain in 1992 by
Belitha Press Limited
31 Newington Green, London N16 9PU

ISBN 1 85561 089 2
Typeset by Chambers Wallace, London
Printed in China for Imago Publishing

British Library Cataloguing in Publication data
for this book is available from the British Library

Acknowledgements

Photographic credits:
Ancient Art and Architecture Collection 1,
    18 centre left
Bridgeman Art Library 5, 21, 25 top
Mary Evans Picture Library 3, 8, 9 top, 12 top and
    bottom, 13 top right, 20 left
Michael Holford 8 centre, 11 top right
Magnum/Eric Lessing 20 right, 23 top
Mansell Collection 13 bottom, 22
NASA 27 top
National Portrait Gallery, London 26
Ann Ronan Picture Library 7 right, 13 top left,
    24 top
Scala 14 bottom, 18/19 bottom, 18 top, 19 top
Science Photo Library 14 top Barney Magrath,
    16 NASA, 17 John Sanford, 18 centre right NASA,
    27 bottom Roger Bessmeyer
Spectrum Colour Library 10 bottom

Cover montage images supplied by Mary Evans
Picture Library, Vivian Fifield, Mansell Collection,
Ann Ronan Picture Library

Illustrations by Tony Smith
Diagrams by Peter Bull

Editor: Kate Scarborough
Designer: Andrew Oliver
Picture research: Juliet Duff

Contents

Introduction   4

Chapter One
The Early Years   6

Chapter Two
The Professor of Mathematics   10

Chapter Three
Studying the Night Sky   14

Chapter Four
Trouble with the Church   19

Chapter Five
The Later Years   22

Chapter Six
After Galileo   26

The World in Galileo's Time   28
Glossary 30
Index   32

Introduction

Science and scientific progress are a vital part of modern life. Inventions such as petrol engines, computers and nuclear power have changed our way of life dramatically. Scientists continue to ask questions, develop their theories, carry out experiments and make new discoveries. Hardly a week passes without news of an important advance in one or other branch of science.

This was not always so. For centuries, areas of science such as physics were seen as part of a general **philosophy** of nature. This had been handed down, unquestioned, from thinkers of ancient times, such as Aristotle and Plato. It also fitted neatly with the ideas of the **Catholic** Church.

Four centuries ago in Italy, Rome was the world centre of the Catholic Christian religion (as it is today). The Church was a powerful force in everyday life. Questioning scientific ideas meant challenging the authority of the Church – which could mean a death sentence.

Galileo was an Italian mathematician, physicist and astronomer who succeeded in changing the course of science. He made great advances in many fields of physics. He championed the ideas of carrying out experiments to test scientific theories, and of using mathematics to study the results. He was the first to look at the night sky with a telescope, and he made many discoveries about the planets and stars.

By encouraging this break from traditional thinking, Galileo paved the way for the scientific progress which has brought us so much today.

During the life of Galileo, Italy was divided into independent city-states. Each main city and its surrounding area was under the control of a wealthy and powerful family, such as the Medici family in Firenze (Florence).

St Peters in Rome –
the heart of the
Catholic Church.

Aristotle and the Church

The Greek philosopher Aristotle, who lived from about 384 to 322 BC, was the main influence on scientific thinking for over 1,800 years.

Aristotle identified two types of motion, called "natural" and "unnatural". In the first type, an object would move up or down. So a stone would naturally fall to the ground and smoke would rise into the air.

Put simply, "unnatural" motion involved moving horizontally – as when a stone is thrown across a field.

In the Heavens, the movements of the stars were natural, but in a different way from on Earth. Their journeys were circular and never-ending, and therefore "perfect" and never-changing.

These ideas, although strange and unscientific now, fitted well with the Catholic Church's teachings in Galileo's time. God was the Creator of all things. The Heavens, being His Works, were perfect, and could not be changed. But on Earth, things were not perfect. People could cause "unnatural" happenings. The power of the Church made it difficult for free thinkers such as Galileo to challenge Aristotle's teachings.

Chapter One
The Early Years

More than 400 years ago in Europe, life was very different from today. There were no factories or industries. Most people worked on farms, or in crafts such as pottery and carpentry. Few children went to school, and even fewer could read and write. Books were rare and very expensive, and they were usually written in **Latin**, the language of scholars and the Church. Science as we learn it today, at school, was almost unknown.

Into this world Galileo Galilei was born on 15 February, 1564, in Pisa, north-west Italy. He had two sisters and one brother. His father, Vicenzio Galilei, was a music teacher. The family was not rich, but Galileo soon showed he was a good student and willing to learn. So, as a young boy, he had a private teacher. The family moved to Florence in 1574, and he was educated by the **monks** of the Camaldolese monastery at nearby Vallombrosa.

The swinging lamp

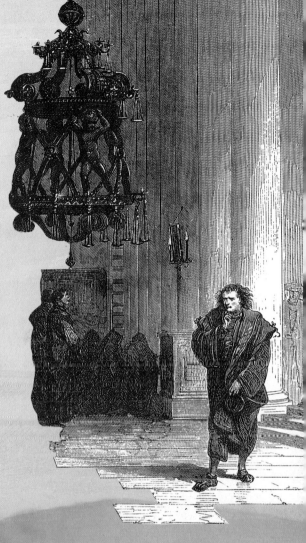

In 1581, while still only 17 years old, Galileo began to study medicine at the University of Pisa. He had vague ideas about becoming a doctor, but his interest in medicine never developed.

It is said that one day in 1581, in Pisa Cathedral, Galileo watched a lamp hung on a long chain from the ceiling. He saw how it swung to and fro in the great, draughty building. He also observed that, whether the lamp swung a long way or only slightly, it took the same amount of time for one complete to-and-fro swing. This observation was not at all what Galileo expected. Later, he happened to overhear a **geometry** lesson at the University. These events began his interest in the branches of science that we now call physics and mathematics. From 1583, he was taught by a family friend, Ostilio Ricci, who lived in Pisa and was a court tutor for the local Duke of Tuscany.

While still only 16 or 17 years old, Galileo saw a chandelier-lamp swinging from the ceiling in Pisa Cathedral. He timed the swings using his pulse as a "clock". Later, he checked his observations by experiments, and made more accurate measurements.

The Italian city of Pisa, in the Tuscany region of Italy, during the late 16th century. Previously the centre of an independent city-state, with a large fleet of ships, it had been taken over by Firenze (Florence), in the 15th century.

Balls, boats and pendulums

In the 1500s, after many centuries of neglect, there was a new interest in the arts, in painting and sculpture, in writing and architecture – and, gradually, in science. This period of new scholarly study is now known as the Renaissance.

Galileo finally left the medical school in Pisa in 1585, partly because his money was running out, and partly because he had lost interest in medicine. Over the next few years he was a lecturer at the Academy of Florence. He also experimented with balls, toy boats, pendulums and many other objects. He watched how they fell, floated and swung. He measured and timed their movements, and tried to devise mathematical explanations for their motions.

By 1586 Galileo had made use of his studies by inventing a new type of hydrostatic balance. This made him famous across Italy and earned him some money. He also wrote a scientific article about the idea that an object has a "**centre of gravity**", which assists calculations about its movements. This helped him to obtain the appointment of Professor of Mathematics at the University of Pisa, in 1589.

This pendulum device meant for keeping time was a design thought up by Galileo the year before his death. It seems that Galileo did not link the swings of a pendulum with time keeping until late in his career.

The arches of the University at Pisa, where Galileo spent four years studying medicine.

Experimental science

The idea of doing experiments was very strange in Galileo's time. For hundreds of years, people had believed the teachings of Ancient Greek philosophers, chiefly Aristotle (see right). No one carried out experiments to check that they were correct. For instance, Aristotle said that heavier objects fall faster than light ones. Galileo carried out many tests on objects falling and rolling down slopes. He showed that two different weights of the same size and shape, dropped at the same time, hit the ground together. By such experiments, Galileo helped to establish the modern approach to science, where ideas and statements are tested to see if they are true.

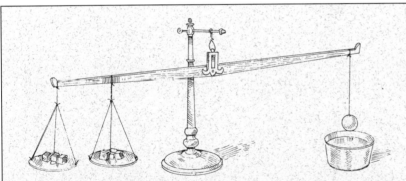

Hydrostatic Balance

This device was based on the principle of **Archimedes**, the famous mathematician who lived 18 centuries before Galileo. An object immersed in a liquid, such as water, weighs less than it does in air, by an amount equal to the weight of water it displaces, or pushes aside.

The balance could identify the metals from which objects were made. It could also find their proportions in alloys, mixtures of metals. This was important because goldsmiths and silversmiths might try to cheat customers, by mixing expensive metals with cheap ones.

The Professor of Mathematics

The Leaning Tower experiment

It is said that, to prove his new ideas, Galileo climbed to the top of the Leaning Tower of Pisa. Watched by teachers and students, he dropped two balls of different weights over the edge. The traditional view was that the heavier ball would hit the ground first. But both balls landed together. Even so, the professors would not listen to Galileo's views. They argued against him and made his life difficult.

Galileo stayed at Pisa for three years. While there, he wrote about moving objects. He studied how they gained speed (accelerated) as they fell or rolled down a slope. He watched how a ball followed a curve when thrown across a courtyard, and he experimented with **levers** and ramps. He always tried to carry out real-life experiments. He measured and timed what happened, and calculated the results mathematically.

Many of his observations did not agree with Aristotle and other ancient philosophers. Galileo's colleagues at the University became angry. They did not believe that anyone should speak out against the traditional teachings.

The Leaning Tower of Pisa, decorated with white marble, was finished in about 1270. It is 55 metres high, so a cannonball dropped from the lower (north) side would hit the ground in less than three seconds.

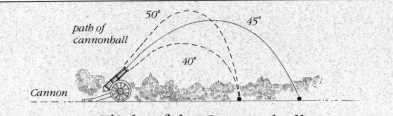

Flight of the Cannonball

In his researches on motion, Galileo rolled cannonballs down planks and measured how they fell to the ground. He noted they did not drop straight down off the plank's end, but fell in a curve, and he measured how far lengthways they travelled from the edge of the plank, and how long they took. The curved path followed by such a cannonball is one type of **parabola**.

Galileo found, from tests and mathematical calculations, that to fire a bullet farthest, the gun should be fired pointing upwards at 45°. He noted that "of other shots, those which exceed or fall short of 45° by equal amounts, have equal ranges".

The thermoscope, designed by Galileo while he was professor at Padova, was used to measure temperature and air pressure.

Professor at Padova

To avoid further conflict, in 1592 Galileo moved to Padova (Padua), near Venezia (Venice), as Professor of Mathematics. Here, the authorities allowed people to speak more freely about their work. Also, they paid more money, but Galileo did not become rich. His father had died in 1591, and he had to take over the family finances. He paid large dowries (wedding gifts) when his two sisters married, and he gave money to his younger brother Michelangelo, who was a musician.

Galileo was Professor at Padova for 18 years. He taught students about geometry and astronomy, and he continued his work on movement and acceleration. He never married, but during his time at Padova, he and his partner Marina Camba had two daughters and a son. He also invented a mathematical instrument, the **proportional compass**, which he sold to help his income. He also studied heat and the effect it has on different liquids. This study led him to develop a simple type of thermometer.

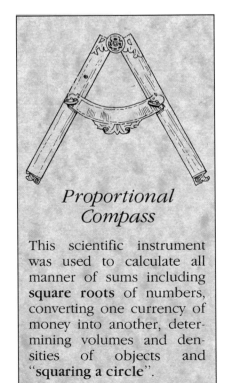

Proportional Compass

This scientific instrument was used to calculate all manner of sums including **square roots** of numbers, converting one currency of money into another, determining volumes and densities of objects and "**squaring a circle**".

Nicolaus Copernicus attended the University of Krakow, in present-day Poland, which was famous at the time for mathematics and astronomy. He also travelled to Italy to study at Bologna, Padova (Padua) and Ferrara. He published his theories of planetary movements in On the Revolutions of the Heavenly Spheres *(1543).*

Copernicus

In about 1597, Galileo read the work of the Polish astronomer Nicolaus Copernicus, who had died more than 50 years earlier. Copernicus had suggested that the Earth and the other planets went around the Sun. This was quite different from the accepted view of the time, which was that everything went around the Earth. It was widely believed that the Earth was the centre of the Universe.

Galileo recognized that the ideas of Copernicus fitted the observations about planetary movements, and they also explained his own theories about how the tides rose and fell on the sea. Galileo had observed that the rhythm of the tides was linked to the movements of both the Moon and the Sun.

Kepler

Copernicus' work had been published by another astronomer and mathematician, Johannes Kepler, who was living in Germany. So Galileo wrote privately to Kepler, saying that he thought Copernicus was right. But he was worried about talking openly, because if he said that the Earth was not the centre of all things, this would go against the traditional teachings and religious views of the day.

Johannes Kepler (1571-1630) was a German astronomer who strongly supported the ideas of Copernicus. He exchanged letters with Galileo, and in 1610 he wrote in praise of Galileo's discoveries with the new telescope.

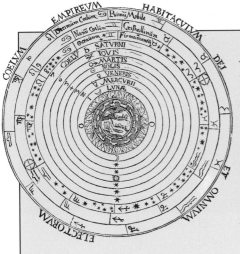

A drawing from 1539 of the solar system, according to the views of ancient scientists such as Aristotle and Ptolemy. The Earth is in the centre. Around it are the 'spheres' or **orbits** *of the six planets known at the time, with their Latin names. The Sun, Solis, is between Venus and Mars. The outermost sphere is* Habitaculum dei, *the Abode of God.*

Two views of the solar system

Ptolemy's view In about the year AD 130, the Greek astronomer Ptolemy improved on the work of Aristotle and described how the Earth, Moon, Sun and other heavenly bodies moved in relation to each other. He believed that the Earth was at the centre, and stayed still. The other bodies moved around it in combined circular paths. This is known as the geocentric system.
Copernicus' system In this system, the Earth was not still. It turned around, once each day. It also moved around the Sun, along with all the other planets. So the Sun was the centre of the Solar System. This theory is known as the heliocentric system. Astronomers have since proved it right.

Ptolemy put forward his geocentric view of the Universe in his book the Almagest, *of about AD 130. He worked out the detailed geometric path for each planet as it moved through the Heavens, with the Earth at the centre. He also produced* Geography, *with maps of the world as it was known at the time. Both books remained popular until the 16th century.*

An early French diagram of the Copernicus system. The Sun is at the centre, with the known planets ranged outwards. Earth is in its correct position, third one out, with the Moon orbiting it. The moons of Jupiter and Saturn are also shown, orbiting their planets. Galileo saw how much better this system fitted in with his observations.

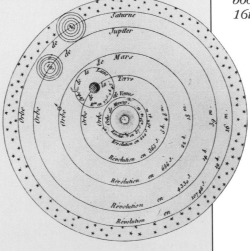

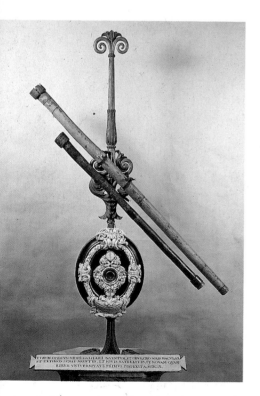

The appearance of three bright comets in 1618 moved Galileo to pursue his study of the Heavens. Above is the famous Halley's comet, which less than a century later, was further proof that Galileo's convictions about the Universe were right. Below are the telescopes used by Galileo to view the stars.

Chapter Three
Studying the Night Sky

In 1604 the sky was lit by a *stella nova* (meaning new star) far away in the Universe. Few people understood what this bright object really was. In reality it was an exploding star, a **supernova**. What it proved to astronomers at the time was that the Heavens, as Aristotle and the Church believed, were not "perfect" and unchangeable. It inspired Galileo to explore his theories on the Universe further.

In 1607 he printed his first book, about the proportional compass he had invented (page 11). Then in 1609 came news from Holland about another invention which had been devised by **Hans Lippershey** the previous year. This was the telescope, a new instrument that used **lenses** to make objects appear much nearer than they were. Galileo began to build his own versions almost at once, and in a few months he had made one that could magnify 32 times. His telescopes were much clearer and more powerful than those of his rivals. They were the first which could be used to study the night sky in detail, and soon they were being used all over Europe.

Galileo received a rich reward. The Venetian governors said he could be Professor for life, and they increased his pay greatly. His financial worries were over.

Galileo showing his telescope and its powers to senior Church officials. Many of these men were very wary of Galileo's claims.

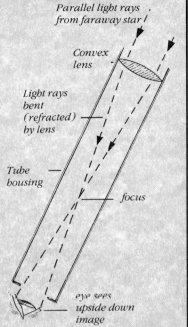

Parallel light rays from faraway star

Convex lens

Light rays bent (refracted) by lens

Tube housing

focus

eye sees upside down image

The Astronomical Telescope

Galileo's telescope used a **convex** glass lens at one end of the telescope to bend or refract the light rays, so that they are brought together and focused into a clear, sharp, magnified, upside-down image at the other end. This principle is still used in modern small telescopes and binoculars.

One reason why Galileo's early telescopes were so successful was that he worked out a new way to check the glass lenses were ground and polished to the correct curvature. This gave magnification without too much blurring or distortion.

A revolution in astronomy

In a few short months of stargazing, Galileo made many important discoveries. He published some of these in his book, *Starry Messenger* (1610).

He saw that the Moon was not smooth, as was thought, but that it had mountains and craters. He realized that the faint milky band across the sky, the Milky Way, was made of millions of separate stars. He saw that the planet Venus had phases, like the Moon, with different parts lit at different times. He also saw moons going around the giant planet Jupiter. He detected dark areas, sunspots, on the Sun. And he could just make out that the planet Saturn was not round but elongated. In fact this shape was due to Saturn's rings.

With his telescope Galileo was the first to notice that Saturn did not look round. Later it was discovered that this was because Saturn has rings.

Sunspots

In 1613, Galileo produced *Letters on Sunspots*, about how and why **sunspots** move across the disc of the Sun. This was his first open support for the Copernican system, suggesting that the Sun

itself rotated, as well as the Earth going around the Sun. He disagreed that the spots were tiny planets orbiting the Sun, as suggested by the German Christoph Scheiner, a Jesuit observer.

The discovery of moons orbiting Jupiter was especially significant. It showed that the Earth was not at the centre of everything, as in Ptolemy's system. Galileo's discoveries caused great argument. Knowing there would be trouble with his colleagues at the University, he decided to move on. He was given the position as court mathematician to the Grand Duke of Tuscany, and he set up home in Florence.

In 1611 Galileo travelled to Rome and showed his telescope to other scientists and important people, including members of the Church. In recognition of his work he was elected to the Accademia dei Lincei. This was the first scholarly scientific society of the modern age, which had only recently been founded in 1603.

Then in 1613 Galileo wrote *Letters on Sunspots*, which was published by the Accademia dei Lincei. The book was based on research done using the telescope with which he had won his award to the Accademia. In his book, for the first time, Galileo openly supported the Copernican system. Events were becoming serious.

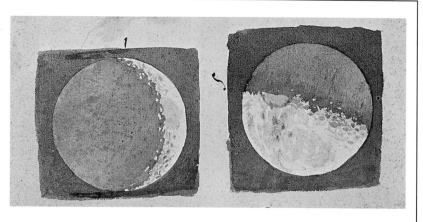

▷ *Galileo was an accurate observer and recorder, as shown by his drawings of the Moon's cratered surface in different phases, from his notebooks. Sadly, many of his documents were destroyed because of his troubles with the Church.*

▷ *The objective (front) lens from one of Galileo's telescopes. Galileo's lenses were mostly a few centimetres across. The largest telescope lens today is the refractor at the Yerkes Observatory, Wisconsin, USA. It measures 102 centimetres in diameter.*

▷▷ *A modern photograph of Io, one of Jupiter's moons. Galileo observed that this giant planet had four "stars" (all planets, moons and stars were known by this name at the time). They are now called the Galilean moons– Io, Europa, Ganymede and Callisto. We have so far discovered a total of 16 moons in orbit around Jupiter, and a satellite ring of rocks.*

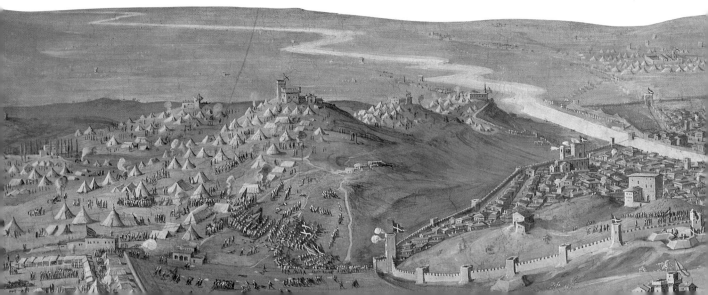

Chapter Four
Trouble with the Church

In Italy in the 17th century, the Church was extremely powerful. People who disagreed with its teachings were seen as **heretics** who should be punished. Galileo knew his views on astronomy would get him into trouble, since the Church believed in the **geocentric** system. So in 1615 he wrote a letter in his defence, now known as the *Letter to the Grand Duchess Christina*.

In this, Galileo argued for freedom for science. He said that scientists should be able to express their thoughts and opinions, and to carry out experiments to prove or disprove their theories. He warned against people simply believing the traditional teachings of those like Aristotle and Ptolemy, without testing them for themselves and making their own observations and measurements. This plea seems strange today, when experiment is such a central part of science. But it was not so in Galileo's time.

The letter did not succeed. Galileo went to Rome and tried to convince Pope Paul V of the need for scientific freedom – and that Copernicus was right. But the Pope was not persuaded. In 1616, a church investigation ordered Galileo never to talk or write in support of Copernicus again, under threat of prison.

Grand Duchess Christina, to whom Galileo wrote in 1615, pleading for freedom of science. The letter was really meant for her son the Grand Duke of Tuscany.

Firenze (Florence), capital of the Tuscany region, in Galileo's day. The city was a world centre for arts, architecture and finance, especially from the 13th to the 16th centuries.

Maffeo Barberini became Pope Urban VIII (1623-44).

Back in Florence, Galileo continued work on physics, motion and mechanics. Some of the results of this work were published in his book *Assayer* (1623). He described how work must begin with the real world, rather than with ancient beliefs. Also in 1623 his old friend Maffeo Barberini became the next Pope, Urban VIII. He allowed Galileo to write a balanced book comparing the old and new astronomical theories. This was the *Dialogue Concerning the Two Chief World Systems* (1632).

The triumph of the Dialogue

The *Dialogue concerning the Two Chief World Systems*, is one of the greatest scientific books. It challenged the teachings that there were two sets of natural laws, one for Heaven and one for Earth.

Galileo put forward the view that the Earth and human beings were not apart from the Heavens. The Earth was a planet, part of the solar system, which was part of an even bigger Universe. Humans and everything else on Earth were subject to natural laws, which the sciences of physics and mathematics could describe. Whether it was a ball thrown into the air, or a planet orbiting the Sun, the same laws applied and science could offer an explanation. The book also contained advances in many other areas of physics.

Most books at the time were written in Latin. Galileo wrote the *Dialogue* in Italian, because he wanted everybody to read and understand his work.

Under arrest!

Galileo's *Dialogue* was first approved by the Church authorities. Upon publication, it was greeted as a masterpiece by scientists and philosophers across Europe.

However, it soon became clear that the book was not evenly balanced. Galileo had decided that the scientific evidence supported the Copernican **heliocentric** system. This meant that much of the accepted scientific knowledge of the time – based on the teachings of Aristotle and the Ancients – must be wrong.

Within a few months, in February 1633, Galileo was back on trial in Rome. The Pope, formerly his friend, was now his enemy. Galileo was accused of breaking his agreement that he would never again support Copernicus and go against the Church and its beliefs. He defended himself strongly in front of the Church **Inquisition**, saying that scientific observations and facts could not be ignored. But in the end, he was forced to admit that he had gone too far. All of his books were banned, and copies of the *Dialogue* were ordered to be burned. Galileo's punishment was prison – for life.

Galileo was prosecuted on "vehement suspicion of heresy", although it is quite possible that some of the documents used as evidence against him, from his previous appearance in 1616, had been "planted". Galileo was made to read out a document admitting he was wrong, and saying the Copernican system was false. At the end, he was supposed to have muttered "Eppur si muove" – "Still it moves" – referring to the Earth moving around the Sun.

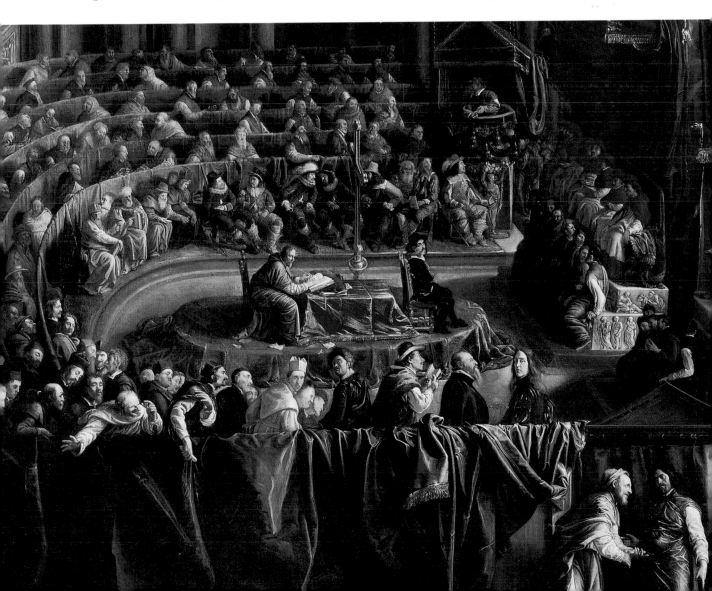

Chapter Five
The Later Years

Galileo was devastated by the punishment of life imprisonment. But the Pope quickly changed this to house arrest. In December 1633, Galileo returned to his home, Villa Arcetri, in the hills near Florence. The house and gardens were his "prison" for the rest of his life.

What do we know of Galileo's personal life? An active and outgoing man, he had many friends, ranging from professors and noblemen, to members of the Church, artists and traders. He loved painting and poetry, and he studied literature so that he could write his own works in a clear and entertaining style. This house arrest must have been very frustrating for him. Even during his later years, as his health gradually failed, he was still not allowed to leave his villa to visit doctors in Florence.

Galileo was sentenced to life imprisonment on 21 June 1633. However the Pope reduced this part of the punishment to house arrest, and by December of that year, Galileo had returned to his villa near Firenze (Florence).

Work at Villa Arcetri

Encouraged by his friend the Archbishop of Siena, Galileo soon returned to work at his home. He continued to write, and his great book *Discourses and Mathematical Demonstrations Relating to Two New Sciences Concerning Mechanics* had to be **smuggled** from Italy because of the ban on his publications. It was printed by Louis Elzevirs at Leiden, Netherlands, in 1638.

Galileo was still a keen astronomer. In 1637 he discovered that the Moon had regular **librations**. These librations look like slight rocking movements made by the Moon and the result means that we can see more than half of the Moon's surface at any one time. The Moon "rocks" because its **equator** is not at right angles to its **axis** of spin and because it does not go around the Earth at a regular speed.

Galileo's villa at Arcetri, where he spent the last nine years of his life. Here he wrote the famous book Discourses, *and carried on his work in physics, mechanics and mathematics. Many scientists and travellers visited the house, since Galileo was now known throughout Europe, chiefly for his earlier works, the "newsletters" of* Starry Messenger *and the* Dialogue.

Two New Sciences

Galileo's last main book was *Discourses and Mathematical Demonstrations Relating to Two New Sciences Concerning Mechanics*. It was a summary of his early experiments and his recent advances in physics, including his work on motion and the strengths of various substances.

Galileo's own view was that the *Discourses* was the beginning of a new era in the physical sciences. This proved so, since it was one of the main influences on the work of Isaac Newton (see page 27).

The great poet John Milton visited Galileo in 1638, on his travels through France, Switzerland and Italy. Galileo was a keen admirer of literature, especially the Roman poet Virgil and the Italian writer Dante (who had also lived in Firenze).

The funeral of Galileo was attended only by family and close friends. His admirers wished for a great service, but they were warned not to offend the Church authorities in Rome.

The next year, Galileo became blind. Yet he remained busy and inventive. He wrote letters to many other scientists. Villa Arcetri was visited by famous people such as his long-time friend the Grand Duke of Tuscany, English poet John Milton, and the English scientist and philosopher Thomas Hobbes. He worked with his pupils Vincenzo Viviani and Evangelista Torricelli, who later became well-known physicists.

The Final Pardon

Attempts were made to obtain a pardon and free Galileo of his house arrest, but these failed. Galileo himself said that he could not expect a pardon, because only the guilty could be pardoned. He was still working on ideas about pendulums, and what happened at the impact when two objects collided, when he suffered a fever. He died at Arcetri on 8 January, 1642.

Galileo's friends and followers, including the Grand Duke, wanted a fitting burial and tomb for such a great man. But the Church Inquisition in Rome still held the view that Galileo was a condemned heretic. So he was buried at a quiet ceremony in the family church, Santa Croce, Firenze (Florence). Only in the next century was he given true recognition. His remains were moved to a fine tomb in the cathedral, and Galileo took his rightful place in history as one of the greatest scientists of all time.

Galileo's tomb as it is today, in Firenze (Florence). The epitaph was written by his pupil Vincenzo Viviani.

Chapter Six
After Galileo

In Italy, after his death, Galileo's colleagues and their pupils carried on his work. Benedetto Castelli began the science of **hydrodynamics**, the study of forces and pressures in liquids. Evangelista Torricelli experimented with air pressure and devised an instrument to measure it, the barometer. Bonaventura Cavalieri worked in mathematics and helped to start the branch of this science called **calculus**.

Galileo's discoveries with the telescope had made him famous as the leading astronomer in Europe. Some scientists did not believe his observations, saying that they were caused by the telescope itself, which was a new and unproven invention. However, over the following years others built telescopes, and they showed that Galileo's early sightings were correct. From this firm footing, astronomy developed as a major branch of science.

Apart from astronomy, Galileo was best known in Europe for his two main books, *Dialogue* and *Discourses*. Because of the Church ban, his writings were forbidden in Italy, although secret copies were available. They were also smuggled to other countries, where they were published. Scientists read them eagerly and developed the ideas.

Isaac Newton (1642-1727) was born the year of Galileo's death. He took up the advances that Galileo had made and in a more receptive society was able to bring about great change in the study of science.

Telescopes and astronomy have changed enormously since Galileo's time. Most of the big modern telescopes are **reflectors**, *using a central mirror, rather than lenses as in Galileo's refractors. The Shane telescope at the Lick Observatory on Mount Hamilton, California, USA, has a main mirror 3 metres across (below). The Space Shuttle, itself an amazing feat of mechanical and electronic engineering (left), launches special telescopes into space. Since these do not have to look through the dusty atmosphere, they can see farther and more clearly into the Universe than any telescope on the planet's surface.*

Galileo hoped that his last book, the *Discourses*, would begin a new era in scientific freedom and investigation. It dealt with various areas of physics such as heat, light and sound. It covered acceleration, falling objects and other aspects of motion and mechanics. It showed how new theories should be tested by experiments, and how mathematics could analyse the results. It even touched on the idea of "infinitesimals", when substances were divided into their smallest possible parts. We know of these today as atoms and elementary particles.

The year Galileo died another great scientist, Isaac Newton, was born. Within thirty years Newton was building on the work of Galileo, the French mathematician and philosopher René Descartes, the English chemist Robert Boyle, and other scientists. In 1687 he published his monumental book, usually called *Principia*, which many experts agree is the greatest scientific work of all time. Helped largely by Galileo, the modern age of science had begun.

The World in Galileo's Time

	1550-1575	1576-1600
Science	1551 Galileo is born 1564 Gessner writes *Historia Animalium*, the first work on animals since the ancients 1569 Gerard Mercator founds the science of cartography, mapmaking	1589 Galileo becomes Professor of Mathematics at Pisa 1590 Zacharias Janssen invents the first microscope
Exploration	1559 Tobacco arrives in Europe from North America 1571 The Portuguese establish a colony in Angola, Africa 1571 The Spanish take over the Philippines	1584 Potatoes are first imported into Europe 1585 John Davis tries to find the North-West Passage: he fails but finds Davis Strait near Greenland
Politics	1562 Wars of Religion begin in France 1563 The Pope creates Cosimo de' Medici Grand Duke of Tuscany 1569 War starts between Denmark and Sweden	1581 The Russians begin their conquest of Siberia 1588 Francis Drake and the English fleet defeat the Spanish Armada 1600 Oyo Empire at its height in Africa
Art	1569 Peter Breughel the Elder dies 1570 Palladio writes his *Treatise on Architecture*	1596 Italian artist Caravaggio completes *The Supper at Emmaus* 1600 First performance of William Shakespeare's *Hamlet*

1604 The supernova awakens Galileo's interests in astronomy; the explosion is also recorded by Johannes Kepler, and by astronomers in China and Korea

1616 Galileo is told never to support the Copernican system by the Inquisition in Rome

1608 Jamestown, Virginia, becomes the first permanent English settlement in North America

1610 The French establish the colony of Quebec in North America

1603 James VI of Scotland becomes James I of England, the first Stuart king

1605 Akbar, third Mogul Emperor of India and one of its greatest rulers, dies

1618 Thirty Years' War starts in Germany and soon spreads to central Europe

1602 Kabuki Theatre begins in Japan

1604 English poet Christopher Marlowe publishes *Doctor Faustus*

1607 *La Favola d'Orfeo* by Monteverdi becomes the first true opera

1633 Galileo again goes before the Inquisition in Rome, and is eventually sentenced to house arrest

1641 Galileo invents the first pendulum clock

1642 Galileo dies

1641 The first live chimp is brought from Africa to Europe, to Holland

1642 Tasman discovers Tasmania and New Zealand

1646 The English occupy the Bahamas

1630 Treaty of Madrid ends war between England and Spain

1633 Charles I of England crowned King of Scotland

1642 English Civil War begins

1644 Ming Dynasty is overthrown in China

1632 Harvard College is founded in Massachusetts, USA, as the first American university

1632 Rembrandt paints *The Lesson in Anatomy of Dr Tulp*

1639 The first printing press is established in North America

29

Glossary

air pressure: the weight of the air in the atmosphere around the Earth, pressing on objects. Air pressure is greatest at sea level, about 1 kilogram per square centimetre. It becomes less as you go higher, up mountains or in a plane, and is zero in space.

Archimedes: one of the greatest mathematicians of ancient Greece. He was born around 287 BC in Syracuse, Greece.

axis: an imaginary straight line that on the Earth passes through the North and South Poles. The Earth spins around this line.

calculus: a branch of mathematics which used calculations and equations to find lengths, areas and volumes, and especially how these change with time.

Catholic: to do with the Roman Catholic Church, which is the largest group within the Christian religion, and has the Pope in Rome as its head.

centre of gravity: an imaginary place where all the weight of an object is concentrated. In most cases the centre of gravity is inside the object; in a ball, it is exactly in the centre. If you could support the object at this point, it would balance perfectly.

convex: curving or bulging outwards. A convex *lens* has two outward-curving surfaces, so that it is fatter in the middle than around the edges.

epitaph: a written passage or speech for a dead person, often on their tombstone, in memory of their life and works.

equator: an imaginary line around the Earth, at its widest point midway between the North Pole and South Pole.

geocentric: when the planets, moons, stars and other heavenly bodies move in various ways around the Earth, which is in the centre and stays still. (See also *heliocentric.*)

geometry: a branch of mathematics which deals with lines, flat shapes such as circles and squares, and solid shapes like spheres and cubes. It uses mathematical equations to find lengths, areas, volumes and other features.

Hans Lippershey: a Dutch scientist who invented an early form of the telescope in about 1608, using two *convex* lenses. A year later he also devised an early type of microscope.

heliocentric: when the planets (including Earth) and their moons move around the Sun, which is at the centre. (See also *geocentric.*)

heretics: people who go against the accepted beliefs and teachings of the Church.

hydrodynamics: the study of pressures, forces and movements in fluids – for example, as in the flow of oil in a car engine.

inquisition: an organization in the Roman Catholic Church which searched out *heretics*. (It lasted from about the 13th to the 19th centuries.)

Latin: the language of Ancient Rome and the Roman Empire. It was used in important speeches and writings by the Church, scholars and educated people in medieval times, but is rare today.

lenses: pieces of transparent material such as glass or plastic, specially shaped to alter the direction of light rays (see also *convex*).

levers: rods, bars or similar long, rigid objects which pivot at one point, the fulcrum, and which can be used for moving heavy weights. A crowbar and a see-saw are types of levers.

librations: oscillations or "wobbles", slight to-and-fro movements. The Moon has librations as it goes around the Earth.

monks: a community of religious men, who dedicate their lives to God.

orbits: the paths traced out by the moons as they go round planets, or planets as they go round stars. The orbits of the Earth and other planets around the Sun are not circles but oval-shaped, or elliptical.

parabola: a particular type of curve, which does not keep bending by the same amount like a circle, but gradually becomes straighter. A stone thrown across a field follows a parabola.

philosophy: the study of human knowledge, beliefs and thoughts. It affects many aspects of our lives, such as how we know things, why we believe in right and wrong, and why we think some things are valuable but others are worthless.

proportional compass: an early type of calculating device, with two arms linked by a pivoted joint. The answer to a calculation was found by moving the arms to a certain position, and reading where the different rows of numbers crossed.

reflector: objects, like mirrors, that are needed to reflect light, sound or heat.

smuggled: when items were taken secretly and against the law from one country to another. This happened with Galileo's books, which were supposed to be banned. Today it happens with drugs and similar illegal substances.

square root: a number which, when multiplied by itself, gives the number you already have. For example, if the number you already have is 4, its square root is 2. The square root of 9 is three.

squaring a circle: finding the length of the side of a square which has the same area as the circle you already have. For a circle 100 millimetres across, a square with the same area has each side measuring 88.6 millimetres.

sunspots: dark areas which move across the surface of the Sun, usually lasting for a few weeks. They are the result of disturbances in the Sun's incredibly powerful magnetic field. Although they look small, they are 20,000 kilometres or more across.

supernova: an exploding star, that suddenly becomes much brighter over hours or days, so that it can be seen even in daylight. It then slowly fades away over days and weeks. Only three supernovae have been recorded in our part of the Universe in modern times in 1054, 1572, and 1604 (the one Galileo saw).

Index

Accademia dei Lincei 17
Almagest (Ptolemy) (AD 130) 13
Archimedes 9
Aristotle (384-322 BC) 4, 5, 9, 10, 13 19
Assayer (Galileo) (1623) 20
astronomy 4, 10, 11, 14-21, 26-7
    planets 16, 18, 20
    telescopes 12, 14, 15, 18, 26, 27
    theories about 12-13, 17, 19, 20-1

balls, experiments with 8, 10, 11
ban on Galileo's books 19, 21, 23
Barbarini, Maffeo *see* Urban VIII, Pope
barometer, the 26
Boyle, Robert 27

calculus 26
Camaldolese monastery 6
Camba, Marina 11
cannonball, flight of the 11
Castelli, Benedetto 26
Cavalieri, Bonaventura 26
centre of gravity 8
Christina, Grand Duchess of Tuscany 19
Church, the Catholic 4, 5, 15, 19-21, 24
    St. Peters, Rome 5
clock, pendulum 8, 29
comets 14
compass, proportional 11, 14
Copernicus, Nicolaus 12-13, 17, 19, 20-1
    map of the Solar System 13

Dialogue (Galileo) (1632) 20,21, 23, 26
Discourses (Galileo) (1638) 23, 26, 27

experimental science 4, 8-9, 10, 11, 19, 27

Firenze 6, 18-19
    the Academy of 8
    Galileo's tomb 25

Galilean moons (Jupiter) 18
Galileo Galilei (1564-1642)
    before the Inquisition 21
    funeral 24-5
    meets Milton 24
    in prison 22
    shows church officials his telescope 15
    and the swinging lamp 7
    tomb in Firenze 25
geocentric planetary system 12-13, 19, 20-1
geometry 7, 11

Halley's comet 14
heliocentric planetary system 12-13, 17, 20-1
hydrostatic balance 8, 9

'infinitesimals' 27
Inquisition, the 21, 25, 29
Io (Jupiter's moon) 18
Italy, map of 4

Jupiter 16, 17
    Io (moon) 18

Kepler, Johannes (1571-1630) 12, 29

lenses 14, 15, 18
Letter to the Grand Duchess Christina (Galileo) (1615) 19
Letters on Sunspots (Galileo) (1613) 17
librations, the Moon's 23
Lippershey, Hans 14

mathematics 4, 7, 23, 26, 27
    Galileo, professor of 8, 10-11, 17, 28
de' Medici, Cosimo *see* Tuscany, Grand Duke of
Milton, John 24
Moon, the 12, 16, 18
    librations of 23
motion, study of 5, 8, 9, 10-11, 20
    Galileo's *Discourses* 23, 26, 27
    see also planets, theories about

'natural' motion 5
Newton, Sir Isaac (1642-1727) 23, 26

On the Revolutions of the Heavenly Spheres (Copernicus) (1543) 12

Padova 11
parabolas 11
Paul IV, Pope 19
pendulums 8, 25, 29
    swinging lamp 7
physics 4, 7, 8-9, 10, 11, 20, 23, 25
Pisa 6-7
    Cathedral chandelier 7

Leaning Tower of 10
    University arches 8
planets, the 4, 5
    Jupiter's moons 18
    Saturn 16
    theories about the 12-13, 17, 20-1
Principia (Newton) (1687) 27
prison, Galileo in 21, 22
Ptolemy 13, 19

reflector telescopes 27
Renaissance, the 8

St. Peters, Rome 5
Saturn 13, 16
Shane telescope (USA) 27
Solar System, the 4, 5, 17
    planets of 16, 18
    theories about the 12-13, 17, 19, 20-1
space shuttle 27
Starry Messenger (Galileo) (1610) 16, 23
sunspots 16, 17
supernova 14, 29
swinging lamp, the 7

telescopes 4, 12, 14, 15, 26
    object lens 18
    Shane (USA) 27
thermoscope (thermometer) 11
Torricelli, Evangelista 24, 26
Tuscany
    Grand Duchess of 19
    Grand Duke of 19, 28

'unnatural' motion 5
Urban VIII, Pope 20, 22

Venus 16
Villa Arcetri 22, 23, 24, 25
Viviani, Vicenzo 24, 25